BEYOND YOUR
RELEASE DATE

Fighting Illegal Detention in
New Mexico's Prisons and Jails

KENNETH H. STALTER

Published by Stalter Law LLC
PO Box 90336, Albuquerque, NM 87199
www.stalterlaw.com

Library of Congress Cataloging-in-Publication Data

Stalter, Kenneth H.
Beyond Your Release Date: Fighting Illegal Detention in New Mexico's Prisons and Jails / Kenneth H. Stalter

ISBN: 979-8-9928381-0-7

Printed in the United States of America
First Edition: 2025

DISCLAIMER

This book provides general information about civil rights claims and legal procedures in New Mexico prisons and jails. While I've worked to make this information accurate and useful, it's not legal advice for your specific situation. The law is complex and constantly evolving. Courts may interpret laws differently over time, and what worked in one case might not apply in another.

Every case depends on its own unique facts and circumstances. What seems like a small detail - a missed deadline, a different facility, a particular policy - can completely change how the law applies. That's why it's crucial to consult with a qualified attorney who can review your specific situation and give you proper legal advice.

Nothing in this book creates an attorney-client relationship. If you believe your rights have been violated, don't rely solely on this book - reach out to an attorney who can evaluate your case properly. The legal principles discussed here may or may not apply to your situation, and only a lawyer who knows the details of your case can tell you where you stand.

Think of this book as a starting point for understanding your rights, not a substitute for legal representation. It's meant to help you spot issues and ask the right questions, but ultimately, protecting your rights requires individualized legal help.

NOTE

All the cases discussed in this book are real cases. I'm using fake names to protect the identities of my clients, but every story in this book is based on a real case handled by my firm. Only the names have been changed—the stories, the wrongdoing by officials, and the strategies my firm used are all real.

ABOUT THE AUTHOR

Kenneth H. Stalter brings experience from every angle of New Mexico's justice system to his civil rights practice. After graduating from Harvard Law School, he served as a prosecutor in Farmington and later as General Counsel for the New Mexico Attorney General's Office. As a special prosecutor the Attorney General's Office, he successfully prosecuted one of the state's highest-profile murder cases.

In 2018, he founded his own firm. Through handling appeals for the Public Defender's Office, he saw firsthand how often incarcerated individuals' basic rights were violated. When New Mexico passed its Civil Rights Act in 2021, he saw a new opportunity for holding prison and jail facilities accountable when they break the rules. His approach combines thorough investigation with strategic legal action to get results for clients who've been wrongfully detained.

CONTENTS

INTRODUCTION

WHEN THE SYSTEM FORGETS YOU

A week before Christmas, a New Mexico judge issued what seemed like a crystal-clear order: Jimmy had "fully completed his sentence in this matter and shall be immediately released from the custody of the New Mexico Corrections Department."

Simple, right? Jimmy had served his time. The judge said he should go home. In America, that should be the end of the story.

But Christmas came and went. New Year's came and went. Jimmy was still sitting in his cell at the Otero County Prison Facility. His family called everyone they could think of - his case worker, prison officials, the records department. Nobody had answers. Or maybe more accurately, nobody cared enough to find the answers.

This wasn't happening in some foreign dictatorship. This was happening right here in New Mexico, in the American justice system. And sadly, Jimmy's case wasn't unique. Every year, people sit in New Mexico prisons for days, weeks, or even months after they should have been released. Sometimes it's because of paperwork delays. Sometimes it's because officials disagree with a judge's order. Sometimes it's simple negligence. But every extra day someone spends behind bars illegally is a day they can never get back.

I've dedicated my career to fighting these injustices, but it's not the path I originally imagined for myself. When I graduated from Harvard Law School, most of my classmates headed to big corporate firms in New York or D.C. I chose a different direction, coming back to New Mexico where I'd been born. I worked as a prosecutor, then for the Attorney General's office, handling everything from DWI cases to first-degree murder trials. That experience showed me how the system really works - both its strengths and its deep flaws.

But it was my work handling appeals for the Public Defender's office that opened my eyes to something crucial: we talk about being a "nation of laws," but too often, the system itself ignores those very laws. I saw case after case where prisons simply didn't follow court orders, didn't properly calculate release dates, or didn't provide basic constitutional protections. When I looked deeper, I found that many of these violations weren't just negligent - they were systemic.

In Jimmy's case, I ultimately had to get creative. When letters to prison officials went unanswered, I took the story to the media. The day after the Albuquerque Journal ran a headline about a man being held despite a judge's release order, Jimmy finally went home. We later proved through emails that prison officials had known about his release order within days of the judge signing it. They just hadn't bothered to act.

That's why I wrote this book. If you're reading this, you might have a loved one in prison who's facing a similar situation. Maybe they've passed their release date. Maybe the prison is ignoring a court order. Maybe you're just worried about making sure everything goes right when their time comes. Or maybe you're an inmate yourself, trying to understand your rights and protect them.

I want to give you practical tools for fighting back when the system fails. We'll look at real cases I've handled, break down what worked and what didn't, and give you specific strategies you can use. You'll learn how to document problems effectively, what deadlines matter most, and when you need to get legal help.

But this book is about more than just practical advice. It's about a fundamental principle: no one is above the law. Not prisoners who break society's rules, but also not prison officials who ignore judges' orders. Not parole officers who think they know better than courts. Not government agencies that treat inmates as numbers instead of human beings.

I believe that if we lose the rule of law - if we accept that some people or agencies can ignore the rules whenever they want - then we risk losing everything that makes our justice system work. Every case I take, every battle I fight over a missed release date or ignored court order, is about holding the line on that principle.

In my years handling these cases, I've learned that success often comes down to three things: documentation, persistence, and understanding your rights. This book will help you with all three. We'll walk through exactly what you need to know, what you need to do, and how to protect yourself or your loved ones when the system fails.

Let's get started.

1

CHAPTER

UNDERSTANDING OVERDETENTION

Vincent had walked out of a Curry County courthouse on a Friday afternoon, a free man. The judge had found legal errors in his old plea agreement and allowed him to enter a new one. Because Vincent had already served all the time possible under the new deal, the judge ordered his immediate release. Simple enough.

The judge told Vincent to check in with the local probation office on Monday morning, just to keep them in the loop. Vincent did exactly what he was told. But when he walked into that probation office, something inexplicable happened - they arrested him. No warrant. No court order. Just a parole officer who decided the judge had "messed up."

Let that sink in for a moment. A judge had literally just ordered Vincent's release. But a parole officer decided they knew better than the judge.

This is overdetention. In its simplest form, it means being held in custody when there's no legal authority to do so. But as Vincent's case shows, these situations are rarely simple.

When Legal Authority Ends

To understand overdetention, you first need to understand something basic about imprisonment in America: the government can only hold someone in custody if they have legal authority to do so. That authority usually comes from:

- A conviction and sentence from a court
- A warrant
- A parole or probation violation with proper procedures followed
- A proper detention order while awaiting trial

When that authority ends - whether because you've served your full sentence, a judge orders your release, or the legal basis for holding you disappears - they have to let you go. Not eventually. Not when they get around to the paperwork. Immediately.

Yet in New Mexico's prisons and jails, we regularly see people held long past when they should be released. Here are some common scenarios:

1. **Ignored Court Orders**: Like Jimmy from our introduction, where the prison simply didn't act on a judge's release order.
2. **Good Time Calculation Errors**: Take Julie's case. By the prison's own math, she had completed her sentence in March. Even adding disputed "absconder time," she was done by mid-May. But they held her until June because they couldn't be bothered to prepare her discharge paperwork.
3. **Agency Overreach**: Like Vincent's case, where parole officers decided they could override a judge.
4. **Paperwork Delays**: Sometimes it's as simple as agencies dragging their feet on processing release documents.

Why Every Day Matters

When I explain these cases to people who haven't dealt with the prison system, they sometimes ask, "What's the big deal about a few extra days?" But imagine being Vincent, sitting in a cell when a judge just said you should be free. Imagine explaining to your kids why you missed Christmas when you were supposed to be home, like Jimmy. Imagine watching your release date come and go with no explanation, like Julie.

Every day of illegal detention is a day someone can never get back. It's missed work opportunities. Missed family moments. And remember - these aren't days someone owes society as punishment. These are days the system is taking illegally.

The Focus of this Book

Let's be clear about what we're focusing on in this book. We're talking about situations where someone has been convicted of a crime, received their sentence, and is now being held in prison longer than that sentence allows. In other words, according to the actual judgment from their case - the official document that says how long they're supposed to serve - they should be out. But for some reason, the prison system isn't letting them go.

This is different from cases where someone is in prison because something went wrong at their trial. Maybe their constitutional rights were violated, or their lawyer was ineffective, or new evidence shows they're innocent. Those situations are serious, and they can be addressed through direct appeals or habeas corpus petitions - legal tools designed to challenge unlawful convictions. We'll talk about those briefly later in the book, but they're not our main focus.

What we're really digging into is what happens when the system fails to follow its own rules about release dates. Maybe they miscalculated good time credits, or ignored a judge's release order, or just dragged their feet on processing paperwork. These aren't cases about whether someone should have been convicted in the first place. These are cases about the prison system holding people past their lawful discharge date - the date when, by law, they're supposed to walk free. It might sound simple, but as we'll see, getting the system to follow its own rules often requires real effort and legal action.

What You Can Do

What we're talking about goes by several names: illegal incarceration, false imprisonment, wrongful detention, or overdetention. I'll usually call it overdetention or illegal incarceration from here on out. But whatever you call it, it's wrong. And the rest of this book will give you specific tools for fighting it. For now, I want you to understand three crucial things:

1. If there's no legal authority to hold someone, their detention is illegal from day one. Don't let anyone tell you a few extra days don't matter.
2. Document everything. Vincent's case became strong partly because we could show each step where officials broke the rules.
3. Don't assume anyone in the system will fix things on their own. In most of my successful cases, it took outside pressure - from families, attorneys, and sometimes the media - to get action.

In the next chapter, we'll look at how the system is supposed to work versus how it actually works. Understanding that gap is crucial to protecting your rights or the rights of your loved ones.

But first, let me be clear about something: fighting overdetention isn't just about getting one person released. It's about holding the line on a basic principle - that in America, the government can't just lock people up without legal authority. Every time we let them get away with it, even for a few days, we weaken that principle for everyone.

That's why these cases matter. That's why every day matters. And that's why you need to understand your rights and be ready to fight for them.

2

CHAPTER

WHEN LAW MEETS REALITY

The Path to Civil Rights: From Prosecutor to Prisoners' Advocate

My path to civil rights work wasn't a straight line. After law school, while most of my classmates headed to corporate firms, I moved back to New Mexico and joined a small firm in Albuquerque. Then I took a chance on a political campaign in California. When the candidate lost, I found myself job hunting in the middle of the global financial crisis - not great timing for a young lawyer.

After months of searching, I finally found an opportunity: an assistant district attorney position in Farmington, New Mexico. It wasn't what I'd planned, but I was excited about getting real courtroom experience. In smaller jurisdictions like San Juan County, that experience comes fast.

Those years in Farmington taught me how the system actually works, from the ground up. I started with DWIs and domestic violence cases, then moved up to felony trials and first-degree murder cases. Every day, I worked with police officers, reviewed their reports, watched how they testified. I saw how cases moved through the system - or got stuck in it. I learned which judges followed the rules strictly and which ones played loose with procedure.

One case from those days sticks with me. A defendant claimed he was incompetent to stand trial. Standard procedure would have been for everyone, including the judge, to simply rely on what he told the forensic evaluator. I did something most prosecutors wouldn't bother with - I listened to all his jail calls. In those recordings, I found him discussing his case in detail with friends, showing he clearly understood the charges and trial process. That thorough investigation revealed his incompetency claim was false.

Years later, that same defendant became one of my biggest referral sources for civil rights cases. He respected that I'd been thorough and willing to dig deep, even though I'd used that thoroughness to prosecute him. When he heard I was handling prisoner civil rights cases, he started sending other inmates my way. He knew I'd give their cases the same careful attention I'd given to prosecuting him.

That prosecution experience shapes how I handle civil rights cases today in three crucial ways:

First, I understand the bureaucracy from the inside. I know how agencies document things, how they communicate (or fail to communicate), and where records tend to get lost or mishandled. When a prison claims they never received a judge's release order, I know exactly where to look for proof that they did.

Second, I learned that most problems in the system don't come from malice - they come from indifference. The parole officer who ignored a judge's release order in Vincent's case probably wasn't trying to be cruel. They just didn't care enough to handle it properly. Understanding this mindset is crucial because it shapes how we fight these cases. Sometimes public pressure works better than legal arguments because it forces officials to care.

Third, my prosecution experience taught me the power of thorough investigation. Just like with the competency claim I mentioned earlier, the truth often lives in the details that others don't bother to check. When I'm investigating an overdetention case now, I'm not just looking at the obvious documents. I'm pulling email records, checking communication logs, comparing timestamps on different agencies' paperwork. I'm looking for the small inconsistencies that reveal the bigger truth.

Later in my career, I moved to the Attorney General's office, handling criminal appeals for the state. This gave me a different perspective - I saw how trial court decisions held up (or didn't) under appellate review. I learned which legal arguments tend to succeed and which ones courts reject. Most importantly, I learned how to frame issues in ways that make judges care about them.

This matters because when I'm fighting an overdetention case now, I'm not just arguing about dates on a calendar. I'm showing judges how the system's failures undermine the very principles of justice they're sworn to uphold. I'm connecting individual cases to the broader constitutional principles at stake.

After I opened my own firm, I started handling appeals on a contract with the Public Defender's office. This was when everything clicked into place. I saw how my clients had been failed not just by their original attorneys, but by the entire system. I read transcripts where public defenders openly told judges they were too overwhelmed to provide effective representation - and judges forced them to trial anyway. I saw how impossible it was to get records from prisons, how grievances went unanswered, and how release dates got miscalculated with no recourse.

Working those appeals showed me something crucial: asking courts to uphold convictions is playing on easy mode. Trying to get them overturned? That's when you learn how the system really works - or doesn't work. I only won reversal for one client out of about a dozen appeals. But every case taught me something about where the system breaks down and how those breakdowns hurt real people.

These experiences gave me a unique perspective on overdetention cases. I understand both sides of the system - how prosecutors think, how corrections officials operate, how public defenders struggle, how judges make decisions. This means when someone comes to me with an overdetention case, I can usually spot the failure points quickly. I know where to look for evidence, which legal arguments will work, and how to frame the issues in ways that courts will understand.

But maybe most importantly, these experiences taught me that following the rules matters - even in prison, even with people who've broken society's rules themselves. Because if we let the system ignore its own rules whenever it's convenient, then we don't really have a justice system at all.

How the System Really Works: Vincent's Case

To understand why "simple" release orders become complicated messes, let's dig deeper into Vincent's case. It shows how quick decisions by officials can cascade into weeks of illegal detention, even when a judge has explicitly ordered someone's release.

Here's how it happened: Vincent had entered a plea agreement years earlier, but the court found legal errors in it. The judge allowed him to enter a new plea deal. By that point, Vincent had already served all the time possible under the new agreement. The math was simple - there was no more legal basis to hold him. The judge ordered his immediate release and told him to check in with the local probation office Monday morning, just to keep them informed.

Sounds straightforward, right? Here's what actually happened:

When Vincent showed up at the probation office that Monday, doing exactly what the judge told him to do, the officers arrested him. No warrant. No court order. Just their own decision that the judge had "messed up." They took him to Curry County Detention Center, which accepted him into custody based solely on the parole officer's word.

Let's break down the chain of failures here:

1. **Parole Officers Overstepping**: They had no legal authority to override a judge's release order. Period. But they did it anyway, probably thinking they were "fixing" what they saw as the judge's mistake.

2. **Detention Center's Failure**: Curry County should never have accepted Vincent without proper paperwork showing legal authority to hold him. When someone shows up saying "I'm here because a parole officer disagreed with a judge," that should set off alarm bells.

3. **NMCD's Response**: When Vincent's defense attorney contacted the corrections department's legal team, they claimed

the judge's order wasn't "compliant with the law" and invented a requirement that Vincent could only be released if the parole board approved a plan. A few days later, they changed their story completely and admitted he shouldn't be in custody.

4. **The Transfer**: While all this was happening, Curry County shipped Vincent to Otero County Prison Facility - which also accepted him without proper paperwork showing why he should be in custody.

At each step, someone could have stopped this train wreck by simply asking: "Where's the legal authority to hold this person?" Instead, everyone just passed the problem along, treating Vincent like a hot potato rather than a human being with constitutional rights.

Here's what makes this case so important to understand: None of these failures happened because someone was especially cruel or wanted to hurt Vincent. They happened because the system is built on a chain of people who:

- Don't want to take responsibility for decisions
- Assume someone else has checked the paperwork
- Think following proper procedure is less important than covering themselves
- Would rather hold someone illegally than risk releasing them too early

This is why I tell clients and families that you can't assume the system will fix its own mistakes. In Vincent's case, we eventually won a settlement, but only after:

- Documenting every step of the illegal detention
- Showing how each agency had failed to follow basic procedures

- Proving there was never any legal basis to hold him
- Building a case that forced them to take responsibility

The lesson here isn't just about one case gone wrong. It's about understanding how the system actually works versus how it's supposed to work. When I was a prosecutor, I saw these gaps from the inside. Now, fighting for prisoners' rights, I use that knowledge to spot the weak points where things break down.

More importantly, I've learned that these cases rarely have just one failure point. It's usually a cascade of small decisions, each one building on the last, until someone ends up sitting in a cell with no legal justification for being there.

This is why documentation becomes so crucial. In Vincent's case, every email, every intake form, every transfer record helped us prove that no one in the chain had bothered to verify their legal authority to hold him. Each piece of paper showed another point where someone could have - should have - stopped and said: "Wait, why are we holding this person?"

A Game-Changer: The New Mexico Civil Rights Act

When the New Mexico Civil Rights Act passed in 2021, it fundamentally changed how we fight these cases. Before, we generally had to sue in federal court under Section 1983, which meant dealing with qualified immunity. Qualified immunity basically means officials can't be held accountable unless there's an almost identical previous case showing their actions were clearly wrong. It's a huge barrier that lets lots of violations slip through the cracks.

Here's why this matters for overdetention cases: Even when someone is clearly being held illegally, officials could argue they weren't sure about some small detail of the situation, so they should get immunity. For example, in Vincent's case, the parole officers might have claimed they weren't sure how to handle a judge's immediate release order when it conflicted with their normal procedures.

The New Mexico Civil Rights Act changed that. It lets us bring these cases in state court without dealing with qualified immunity. Plus, it makes the government agency responsible, not individual officers.

Let me show you how this works in practice. Remember Julie's case? She was held months past her release date because officials "couldn't be bothered" to prepare her discharge paperwork. Under the old system, they might have argued qualified immunity because there wasn't a specific case saying exactly how quickly they had to process releases.

Under the Civil Rights Act, we just had to prove two things:

- Her constitutional rights were violated (being held without legal authority)
- The agency was responsible for that violation

That's it. No immunity games. No arguing about whether the right was "clearly established." Just the basic question: Did they have the right to hold her? If not, they're liable.

In Jimmy's case, which came before the Civil Rights Act, we had to get creative. When the prison ignored the judge's release order, we couldn't just focus on the simple fact that they were holding him illegally. We had to anticipate qualified immunity defenses and find similar previous cases. That's partly why we went to the media - we needed to create pressure because our legal tools weren't as strong back then. We later won a settlement as well – but I can't help but wonder if we would have done better if the Civil Rights Act had existed at the time.

The Act also helps with patterns of violations. If an agency repeatedly makes the same mistakes with release dates or ignores court orders, we can use that pattern to show systemic problems. This puts pressure on them to fix their procedures instead of just settling individual cases.

For families dealing with overdetention right now, here's what you need to know about the Civil Rights Act:

1. You have stronger legal tools available than ever before
2. You don't have to prove the exact same thing happened in a previous case
3. The focus is on the basic question: Is there legal authority to hold someone?
4. Documentation is still crucial - but you're documenting the violation itself, not trying to match it to previous cases

Now, this doesn't mean these cases are easy. We still have to prove every element of the violation. We still have to follow proper procedures and meet deadlines. But the Civil Rights Act removed one of the biggest barriers that used to stop these cases before they could even get started.

Why "Simple" Release Dates Become Complex

Let's talk about why something that should be straightforward - letting someone out on their release date - often turns into a mess. It comes down to how the system is built, with multiple agencies involved and nobody feeling truly responsible for getting it right.

Take a typical state prison case. Just to figure out someone's release date, you need:

- The original judgment and sentence from the court
- Good time calculations from the prison
- Any disciplinary records that might affect good time
- Records of time served in county jail before prison
- Parole records and calculations
- Documentation of any program credits

Each of these pieces might come from a different agency or department. Each has their own procedures, their own timelines, their own way of calculating things. And here's the kicker - they often don't talk to each other effectively. Even the judgment and sentence from the court may not accurately include all presentence credit from time served pending trial.

I saw this clearly in Julie's case. According to the prison's own math, she should have been released in March. Even if you counted disputed "absconder time," she was done by mid-May. But the actual holdup? The Parole Board and NMCD couldn't get their act together to prepare a simple discharge certificate. They had all the information they needed. They just didn't make it a priority.

This is why I tell clients and families to start planning for release early. Get copies of everything. Track down each piece of documentation yourself. Don't assume different departments are sharing information, even within the same facility.

I remember one case where the prison's own internal emails showed the case manager knew the person needed to be released, but the legal department wouldn't sign off. Nobody wanted to take responsibility for making the final call. It's easier for them to do nothing than to risk releasing someone "too early." Unfortunately, officials have become accustomed to not being called out.

Here's what makes this even more frustrating: The law says they can't hold someone without legal authority. But in practice, the system is built to default to keeping people in custody when there's any doubt or confusion. They figure it's safer to hold someone an extra week while sorting out paperwork than to risk letting them out a day early.

This backwards thinking shows up in how they handle court orders too. Remember Vincent's case - when a parole officer didn't like a judge's release order, they just ignored it. The detention center accepted some-one into custody without proper paperwork because, in their minds, holding someone illegally was less risky than following a judge's order they didn't understand.

That's why documentation becomes so crucial. Every case I've won started with proving exactly when the legal authority to hold someone ended. We get:

- Court orders with clear dates
- Prison calculations showing sentence completion
- Email trails showing who knew what when
- Grievances filed by the inmate
- Records of family members trying to get answers

When you can lay out this paper trail, it becomes harder for agencies to hide behind confusion or bureaucracy. You can show exactly when they crossed the line from legal detention to illegal imprisonment.

The system won't fix these problems on its own. There's no incentive for change when keeping someone too long has no consequences, but letting someone out "early" might make the news. That's why these civil rights cases matter - they're often the only way to make agencies care about getting release dates right.

The next chapter will give you specific tools for documenting these issues effectively. But for now, understand that no release date is truly "simple" in New Mexico's prison system. The only way to protect your rights is to assume things will get complicated and prepare accordingly.

3

BUILDING YOUR DEFENSE BEFORE YOU NEED IT

Getting Started: Why Preparation Matters

I'm going to be very direct here: The time to start protecting your rights is long before you think you need to. If you wait until there's a problem with your release date, you're already behind. Let me explain why through a recent case.

Last year, a family contacted me about their son who was being held past his release date. They had all his paperwork showing he should be out. They'd called everyone they could think of at the prison. But when I asked if he'd filed grievances about the issue, they looked confused. When I asked for copies of their communications with prison officials, they had nothing in writing. When I asked about his good time figuring sheets, they didn't have copies.

Were his rights being violated? Maybe. Could I help him? I wouldn't know until I got all the records. That could take weeks and their son would be waiting in the meantime.

Here's what you need to understand: Prisons run on paperwork. Every decision, every calculation, every movement is supposed to be documented somewhere. But that documentation only helps you if you can access it when you need it. And in New Mexico's prisons, paperwork has a funny way of disappearing when it matters most.

That's why I tell every client and family to treat documentation like insurance. You hope you never need it, but if you do need it, you need it badly. Here's what that means in practice:

1. Get copies of everything related to your sentence:
   - Judgment and sentence from the court
   - Good time figuring sheets
   - Disciplinary records
   - Program completion certificates
   - Any court orders or modifications
2. Start an organized filing system:
   - Keep originals safe and make copies
   - Date everything, even handwritten notes
   - Create a timeline of important dates and events
   - Save every piece of communication with prison officials
3. Learn your facility's policies:
   - Get copies of grievance procedures
   - Understand good time calculation rules
   - Know your rights regarding medical care and programs
   - Document when policies aren't followed

But here's the crucial part: You need to do this systematically and start early. Too often, families contact me after a problem appears, and we have to reconstruct what happened from memory. That's much harder than having contemporaneous documentation.

Think of it this way: If you're reading this book, you or someone you care about is in the system. The system has tremendous power over lives and freedom. The only way to fight that power is with documentation that proves what really happened.

I'll give you a concrete example. We won Jimmy's because we had concrete proof the prison got the judge's release order within days of it being signed. When prison officials claimed they were "working on it," we had weeks of emails showing they were doing nothing.

That kind of documentation doesn't just help win cases - it can prevent violations from happening in the first place. When prison officials know you're keeping records, they're more likely to follow the rules. When they know you have copies of everything, they can't claim paperwork was lost.

In the next sections, we'll get into the specifics of what to document and how to document it effectively within prison constraints. But right now, I want you to understand three basic principles:

1. Start immediately. Don't wait for problems to appear.
2. Document everything, even things that seem minor. You never know what might become important later.
3. Keep copies outside the prison. Paperwork has a way of disappearing during transfers or searches.

Remember: The system has lawyers, paperwork, and time on its side. The only way to level the playing field is to build your defense before you need it.

Documentation Strategies That Actually Work

Prison documentation is a challenge. You're working with limited resources, restricted access to copies, and rules about what you can keep in your cell. You need strategies that work within these constraints.

I learned this lesson from an unlikely source - the defendant I mentioned earlier who later became a client. When I was prosecuting him, I used his recorded jail calls to disprove his competency claim. Years later, when he became my client, he showed me how he'd learned to document everything about his case. He kept a simple notebook with dates, times, and details of every interaction. Each conversation with staff, every calculation of his time, every promise made about his release date - all recorded in plain, clear language.

That's really all good documentation needs to be. One of my most successful clients kept a small notebook where he'd write entries like: "March 15, 9:30 AM - Talked to Ms. Johnson (Case Manager) about missing good time from county jail. She said she'd look into it. Sent follow-up request next day." Simple, but it tells us who, what, when, and how they responded.

For families on the outside, I recommend creating a basic filing system. Keep copies of everything your loved one sends you. Save emails showing when you contacted the prison. Keep phone records. But don't get caught up in creating the perfect system - just make sure you're saving everything in a way that you can find it later. A simple set of labeled folders can go a long way.

Here's what matters most: Get things in writing whenever possible. If staff tell you something important, ask for it in writing. Keep copies outside the prison - mail them to family or a trusted friend.

Strong documentation completely changes the game. Instead of getting into debates about who's telling the truth, we can point to concrete evidence that shows exactly what happened. Maybe it's a dated grievance form that proves you complained about the issue right away. Or surveillance footage that captures the incident. Or medical records that show you weren't getting prescribed medication. When we have that kind of independent evidence, it doesn't matter if you have prior convictions on your record - the facts speak for themselves. The prison can't just dismiss your complaint by saying "well, this person isn't credible because they're a convict." They have to actually address what the evidence shows.

Think of it like this: If you tell me the prison ignored a judge's release order, that's one thing. But if you can show me the judge's order, the grievances you filed about not being released, and the records showing you were still in custody weeks later - now we're not just talking about your word against theirs. We're talking about documents that tell the story all by themselves. That's why I tell every client: document everything, keep copies of everything, and mail copies to someone on the outside. The stronger your paper trail, the less anyone can try to discredit you based on your record.

Here's the important flip side of what we just discussed:

I'm emphasizing documentation because it makes cases stronger, but don't let perfect be the enemy of good. If your rights were violated, but you're missing some paperwork or didn't file every grievance exactly right - that's okay. Talk to an attorney anyway. Work with what you have. The goal isn't to be perfect - it's to build the strongest case possible with whatever evidence is available.

Think of documentation like building a foundation for your house. The stronger that foundation, the better. But even if there are some cracks or weak spots, you can still build something solid. A missing document might make things more challenging, but it's rarely a deal-breaker. What matters most is that you take action and keep pushing forward. Get help, gather what evidence you can, and don't give up just because the documentation isn't perfect.

The Grievance Process: Your Most Important Tool

I understand that filing grievances might feel pointless. It often seems like they disappear into a black hole. But in the world of prison civil rights, grievances are absolutely crucial. Here's why.

For many types of claims, you literally cannot file a lawsuit unless you've gone through the grievance process first. It's called "exhausting your administrative remedies," and courts take it seriously. The law books are full of strong cases thrown out simply because the prisoner didn't file grievances properly.

But here's something most people don't understand: The value of grievances isn't just about checking a legal box. Every time you file one, you're creating evidence. You're forcing the facility to either respond to your complaint or document that they ignored it. Either way, you're building your case.

Here's how to make grievances work for you:

First, get a copy of your facility's grievance policy. Read it carefully. Follow it exactly. The deadlines in these policies can be incredibly short - sometimes just a few days to file. Missing a deadline can sink your whole case before it starts.

Second, stick to facts in your grievances. Don't include legal arguments or accusations. Just lay out exactly what happened, when it happened, and what you want done about it. For example, instead of writing "My constitutional rights are being violated," write "I was supposed to be released on March 15. It is now March 20. I am being held past my release date." See the difference?

Third, keep copies of everything - the grievance itself, any responses, your appeals. If the facility won't give you copies, write down the grievance word for word in your notebook before submitting it. Mail copies to your family or trusted friend. At my firm, we scan and save any paperwork prisoners send us – even if we don't have an active case.

I handled a case recently where the prison claimed they never received my client's grievances about being held past his release date. But his family had copies of every grievance, complete with staff signatures showing they were received. That documentation turned a potential dismissal into a settlement.

Here's another crucial point: File grievances early and often. Don't wait until you've already been held past your release date. Start documenting concerns as soon as you notice problems with your time calculations or release planning. Create that paper trail before the crisis hits. When you get to court, that paper trail can be the difference between a quick dismissal and a nice settlement.

The system is designed to make you feel powerless. Grievances are one of the few tools you have to force the system to acknowledge problems and document its own failures. Use them.

Building a Paper Trail That Matters

Let me share something I've learned from years of handling these cases: It's not just about having documentation - it's about having the right documentation that tells a clear story. Let me show you what I mean.

Like I said, we can think about building a paper trail like building a house. It doesn't have to be perfect but you want a solid foundation - those basic documents that establish your release date and sentence calculation. Then you build up from there, documenting every problem, every conversation, every attempt to fix things through proper channels.

Here's what a strong paper trail looks like in practice. The most successful cases start with:

- The original judgment and sentence
- Good time figuring sheets, showing the progression of time calculations
- Grievances filed about calculation errors, with responses
- Emails from family to prison officials asking for clarification
- Records showing when the facility received updated court orders
- Documentation of every attempt to resolve the issue internally

When you have that kind of thorough documentation, it tells a story that's hard for prisons to dispute. It shows this isn't just someone complaining - it's a clear pattern of the system failing to follow its own rules.

But here's what's crucial: This kind of documentation doesn't happen by accident. You have to be systematic about it. Every time you get a new time calculation, save it. Every time you file a grievance, keep a copy. Every time you get a response about your release date, document it.

Remember Julie's case? She won because we could show exactly when her sentence should have ended and how long officials dragged their feet on her discharge paperwork. The paper trail proved it wasn't just a delay - it was deliberate indifference to her rights.

In the next chapter, we'll talk about what to do when things actually go wrong. But remember this: The cases I win almost always start with clients who documented everything, even before they knew they'd need a lawyer. They treated every piece of paper like it might matter someday. Because eventually, it probably will.

The system counts on people getting frustrated and giving up. It counts on paperwork getting lost and memories fading. Don't let that happen. Document everything. Save copies. Build your paper trail. Because when you need it - and I hope you never do - you'll be glad you did.

The Bottom Line

Let me be direct: Prison civil rights cases are won or lost on documentation. Not fancy legal arguments. Not dramatic courtroom speeches. Documentation.

Remember: The system has the power. Documentation is how you fight back. It's how you turn a complaint into a case. It's how you prove your rights matter.

In the next chapter, we'll talk about what to do when things go wrong. But everything works better if you've laid this groundwork first.

4
CHAPTER

WHEN THINGS GO WRONG: FIRST STEPS

Understanding Release Dates

When you're incarcerated in New Mexico, release dates can feel like moving targets. Let's clear up some common confusion about when someone should actually get out.

First, here's the most important thing to understand: There's a big difference between your parole date and your discharge date. Your discharge date is when your entire sentence ends - that's the date that really matters. Your parole date is different. Even when you hit your parole date, New Mexico law allows what's called "in house parole." This means the prison can keep you in custody until your discharge date, even if you've reached your parole date.

Here's a real-world example: Let's say you received a sentence of 10 years, with the last 2 years on parole. You might think that means you'll get out after 8 years. But under New Mexico's "in house parole" system, the parole board can keep you in custody for those last 2 years. They don't have to release you until you hit your discharge date - when those full 10 years are up.

This creates a lot of confusion. I've had many people contact my office believing they're being held illegally because they weren't released on their parole date. But unless you have a specific court order requiring your release, or you've hit your final discharge date, being held on "in house parole" is legal under New Mexico law. I disagree with that as a matter of principle, but for now, it's what the courts have said.

So when should you be concerned? Here are the dates that matter:

1. Your discharge date - when your entire sentence (including parole) ends
2. A specific release date ordered by a judge
3. A date when all your charges have been dismissed or resolved

If you're held past any of these dates, that's when you might have a real overdetention case. Everything else - parole dates, expected release dates, even dates that officers or case workers might have mentioned to you - those aren't legally binding.

This system can feel unfair, especially when you've been counting down to a parole date that doesn't end up meaning what you thought it meant. But understanding these distinctions helps you focus your energy on the dates that actually matter legally.

One important note: Parole violations are their own category. If you're accused of violating parole, the parole board has broad authority to impose sanctions or revoke your parole entirely. As long as they follow their own procedures, these actions are generally legal - even if they seem harsh or unfair.

The bottom line? Don't assume you have an overdetention case just because you weren't released on your parole date. But if you're being held past your discharge date, or if a judge has specifically ordered your release, that's when you need to take immediate action. We'll talk about those steps next.

Real Violations vs. Frustrating Delays

One client contacted me furious because he'd reached his parole date with an approved housing plan, but the prison kept him in custody. He was sure this was illegal detention. But when I reviewed his paperwork, he still had two years until his discharge date. The parole board was legally allowed to keep him in custody. Understanding this saved him from spending money on a lawsuit he couldn't win.

Let's be direct about what makes a real overdetention case. The prison system has plenty of frustrating delays and problems, but not all of them create legal claims. Here's how to tell the difference.

Clear Signs of Illegal Detention

1. **Past Your Discharge Date.** When your entire sentence is finished - including any parole time - that's your discharge date. If they keep you even one day past this, that's illegal. I handled a case where my client Julie was held a month past her discharge date because NMCD and the Parole Board dragged their feet on paperwork. That's the kind of clear violation we can fight.

2. **Ignoring a Judge's Order.** Remember Jimmy's case? The judge ordered his immediate release, but NMCD just sat on the order through Christmas. When a judge says "release immediately,"

that means exactly what it sounds like. Any delay beyond basic processing is illegal.

3. **After Charges are Dismissed.** Once charges are dismissed, there needs to be a new charge or valid warrant or detainer to hold you.

4. **Refusal to Hold Required Parole Hearings.** Some sentences, especially for parolees convicted of sex offenses, require the parole board to hold hearings at specific times to review whether continued parole is necessary. I had a client, Michael, who was supposed to get these hearings starting at his five-year mark. The parole board just decided not to hold them. That's illegal - when the law requires a hearing, they can't just skip it because they don't want to do it.

What Usually Isn't Illegal (Even Though It Feels Wrong)

1. **"In House" Parole.** Being held in custody during your parole period feels awful, but it's generally legal. As long you've had the hearing the law says you get, the parole board has the power to make you serve parole in prison.

2. **Parole Sanctions.** The parole board has broad power to impose sanctions if they think you've violated parole. As long as they follow their procedures and don't go past your discharge date, these sanctions are usually legal.

3. **The Parole Board Not Approving a Plan.** The parole board has wide latitude to approve or deny your parole plan. Maybe you want to live with your cousin, but they say no. Or they reject the halfway house you proposed. As long as they're actually

reviewing plans and following their own policies, that's usually legal - even if it means you stay in custody longer. What's not legal is if they simply refuse to review plans at all or apply rules that don't actually exist.

What Creates a Grey Area That Needs Investigation:

1. **Failure to Hold Required Parole Hearings.** When the law requires specific hearings, like in Michael's case where he was supposed to get reviewed at the five-year mark, skipping those hearings is definitely wrong. But that doesn't automatically mean your detention becomes illegal. The courts look really carefully at the specific facts: Would the hearing likely have changed anything? What actual harm came from missing it? How long was the delay? We've had some success challenging these cases, but each one depends heavily on its own circumstances.

2. **Miscalculated Good Time Credits.** If the prison makes a mistake calculating your good time, that could be illegal detention - but we need to look carefully at the math and the policies. Sometimes what looks like a mistake is actually them following a policy you didn't know about. For example, good time credits can change if there's a finding that you absconded from parole. Even if your offense entitles you to day-for-day credit, you may be required to serve 85% of your time after absconding.

3. **Delays in Processing Release Paperwork.** A day or two to process release paperwork is normal. But when it stretches into weeks with no explanation, like in Julie's case, that crosses the line. The tricky part is proving whether the delay

was just bureaucratic slowness (probably legal) or deliberate foot-dragging (illegal).

This is why getting legal help matters so much. These grey areas are where having someone who really knows the case law can make a difference. We need to look at exactly what happened, what the current law says about it, and whether we can prove actual harm. Sometimes what feels like it should be a slam-dunk case turns out to be more complicated - but that doesn't mean you shouldn't explore your options.

Getting Help from an Attorney

Let me be direct about what makes a civil rights case work, because I want to save you time and energy. When someone contacts my firm about a potential case of overdetention, we're going to need three things right away: your judgment and sentence, your good time figuring sheets, and any court orders about your release. Without those basics, we're just guessing.

Here's what happens a lot: Someone writes to me saying they're being held illegally. But when I ask for these documents, they can't get them, or the documents tell a different story. Remember what we talked about earlier - the difference between parole dates and discharge dates? Those documents help us figure out which date matters in your case.

Think of it like building a house. Those basic documents are the foundation. Without them, we can't even start construction. With them, we can figure out pretty quickly if you have a case worth pursuing.

Now, let's talk about red flags when you're looking for an attorney. If a lawyer promises you immediate results or guarantees they can get you out, be skeptical. These cases are complex. Any attorney who doesn't want to review your documents before making promises either doesn't understand prison civil rights work or isn't being straight with you.

Here's what good legal help looks like: An attorney who asks detailed questions about your situation. Who wants to see your paperwork before making any promises. Who explains what they can and can't do for you. Sometimes the most valuable thing I do for potential clients is explain why they don't have a case - it saves them time and energy they can focus elsewhere.

When you're reaching out to attorneys, be specific about what's happening. Instead of saying "They're holding me illegally," say "I was supposed to be released on January 15 according to my judgment and sentence, but I'm still here on February 1." That helps us understand quickly whether we might be able to help.

And be ready for some tough conversations. Sometimes what feels deeply unfair isn't actually illegal. Sometimes what is illegal isn't worth pursuing because the evidence isn't there. A good attorney will be straight with you about these realities.

Here's what I tell every potential client: I can't promise I'll take your case, but I can promise to look at it carefully and give you an honest answer about whether I think there's a legal path forward. Sometimes that means telling people they need to keep working through administrative channels. Sometimes it means explaining why their situation, though frustrating, isn't a civil rights violation. And sometimes it means saying "Yes, this is exactly the kind of case we handle - let's get started."

The right attorney for these cases isn't necessarily the one who tells you what you want to hear. It's the one who helps you understand exactly where you stand and what your real options are. Because at the end of the day, what matters isn't just whether you have a case - it's whether you have a case that can actually achieve something meaningful for you.

5

CHAPTER

THE INVESTIGATION PROCESS

From Harvard to Farmington: Learning How the System Really Works

L et me tell you about how I learned to investigate cases, because it's probably not the path you'd expect.

I graduated from Harvard Law School in 2008. They say you can do anything with a Harvard Law degree, and in some sense that's true, but the school was basically a conveyor belt pushing graduates toward big corporate firms in New York, D.C., and L.A. About ninety percent of my classmates took that path. While they were drafting merger documents in Manhattan skyscrapers, I was trying DWI cases in a single-story magistrate court in Farmington, New Mexico.

Here's what I learned through all of this: The truth lives in the details that most people don't bother to check. When I investigate an over-detention case now, I'm not just looking at the obvious documents. I'm pulling email records, checking communication logs, comparing timestamps on different agencies' paperwork. I'm looking for the small inconsistencies that reveal the bigger truth.

The Harvard law professors taught me how to think about abstract legal theory. But it was those years in Farmington, handling everything from petty crimes to murder cases, that taught me how to really put a case together. How to spot when something doesn't add up. How to find evidence others miss. How to build cases that stand up under pressure.

That's why I tell clients and families: Don't give me theories. Give me documents. Give me dates. Give me names. Give me emails. Because I've learned that winning these cases isn't about clever legal arguments - it's about proving exactly what happened, who knew about it, and when they knew it.

This is why I spend so much time investigating cases before I take them. My prosecution experience taught me that even seemingly simple cases can have hidden complexities. My defense work showed me how crucial details often get overlooked. And my civil rights work has proven that thorough investigation before filing makes all the difference in getting results for clients.

Why I Only Take Cases I Believe In

Let me be direct about something: I turn down a lot of cases, far more than I take. Not because the person hasn't been wronged, but because I need to be certain I can actually help them before I take their case.

Here's a recent example. A prospective client came to me wanting to challenge the length of his parole and the state's failure to credit his parole time. On the surface, it looked like he might have a case. But when

I dug deeper, I found he had waived his parole hearing and admitted to absconding from parole - even though the state's evidence of absconding was pretty thin. Once he made those admissions, my hands were tied. I couldn't help him, even though he probably shouldn't have admitted to absconding in the first place.

One of the hardest types of cases to turn down are those where there's a clear legal violation, but the mistake was made by a judge. I've seen cases where judges made obvious errors that kept someone in prison too long. But judges have absolute immunity for their judicial acts. That means even if a judge clearly messed up, I can't get compensation for my client. The most I can do is try to correct the error going forward.

This is why I spend so much time investigating cases before I take them. I need to know not just that something went wrong, but that I can actually do something about it. That means:

- The violation needs to be provable with solid evidence
- The responsible party needs to be someone we can hold accountable
- The claim needs to fit within the legal deadlines
- There needs to be a real remedy available

Taking cases I can't win doesn't help anyone. It wastes the client's time and gives them false hope. It burns resources that could help someone else. And it can actually make things worse by creating bad precedent that hurts future cases.

This is why I'm brutally honest with potential clients. If I don't think I can help them, I tell them directly. If I'm not sure about something, I say so. Too many lawyers promise the moon because they want the case. I'd rather lose business by being honest than make promises I can't keep.

Some lawyers might say I'm too selective. But I believe my clients deserve an attorney who's fully committed to their case and confident in the strategy. Every case I take gets my complete attention and effort because I know we have a real chance of winning.

The system is already stacked against prisoners trying to protect their rights. Filing weak cases just makes it worse. When I bring a case, I want judges to know I've done my homework and believe in the merits. That reputation helps all my clients, because courts know I don't waste their time with frivolous claims.

Beyond Box-Checking: How I Investigate Cases

Let me tell you about one of my most powerful investigative tools: New Mexico's Inspection of Public Records Act (IPRA). It's not just about getting documents - it's about creating accountability and sometimes even finding additional ways to help clients.

Here's how I use it: When someone contacts me about a potential civil rights violation, I immediately start filing IPRA requests. I want to see everything - emails, incident reports, policy documents, video footage if it exists. But here's the interesting part: Sometimes the agencies' failure to properly handle these records requests becomes a case in itself.

I recently had a series of cases against the Parole Board because they simply weren't responding to records requests. They ended up paying a significant settlement. More importantly, they completely overhauled how they handle records requests. Now other inmates can actually get their records when they need them.

My approach to these investigations is systematic - something I learned getting my master's degree in cybersecurity. I look for vulnerabilities in how agencies handle information. Where do they store records? How do they track communications? What happens to documents during transfers between facilities? Understanding these systems helps me find evidence others might miss.

Let me give you a concrete example. In one case, NMCD claimed they never received a judge's release order. Through IPRA requests, I found emails proving not only that they received it, but that they'd internally discussed ignoring it. That documentation turned a civil rights case into a settlement.

I've even taken on private prison operators like Management & Training Corporation (MTC) over whether their records are public. Think about it - they're performing a government function using taxpayer money. Shouldn't the public have a right to see their records?

Some government attorneys have accused me of turning IPRA into a "cottage industry." One NMCD attorney even made that argument in court. He's since retired, and his replacement quickly changed course and settled the case. Because here's the truth: If agencies followed the law and provided records when asked, there wouldn't be any IPRA cases to bring.

This is why I teach other attorneys how to use IPRA effectively. It's not just about getting documents - it's about using the law to force transparency in a system that prefers to operate in shadows. Every time we win an IPRA case, we make the system a little more accountable.

In Julie's case, my initial IPRA requests showed the prison was dragging its feet on her release paperwork. When they failed to provide all the records we requested, that became another claim we could bring. The IPRA violations actually helped prove the underlying civil rights case by showing a pattern of indifference to her rights.

Building Trust Through Straight Talk

Let me tell you about a conversation I had recently with an incarcerated client. He asked me a complex question about how a particular law might apply to his situation. I told him simply, "I don't know the answer to that." He paused for a moment, then said "Thank you for saying that." He explained that he'd dealt with too many attorneys who made up answers just to sound smart.

That moment captures my whole approach to client relationships. I don't need to pretend I have all the answers. I have a Harvard Law degree hanging on my wall - I don't need to prove I'm smart. What I need to do is be honest with my clients about what I can and can't do for them.

Here's how this plays out in practice. When someone comes to me with a potential case, I'm direct about three things:

1. Whether I think I can help them
2. What exactly I'll need to prove
3. What challenges we're likely to face

Remember what I said earlier about only taking cases I believe in? That starts with honest conversations. Sometimes I have to tell people, "Yes, you were wronged, but because of judicial immunity, I can't help you." Or "This is clearly unfair, but we don't have the documentation to prove it."

I've found that clients and their families appreciate this directness, even when the news isn't good. Many of them have dealt with attorneys who promised the moon but delivered nothing. They've had enough empty promises. They want someone who will shoot straight with them.

Take Vincent's case. When his family first contacted me, I told them exactly what we'd need to prove - that he was held without legal authority and that the responsible parties knew it. I explained what evidence we'd look for and what hurdles we might face. By being clear about the process from the start, they understood both the strength of their case and why certain steps were necessary.

This straight talk becomes especially important when we're investigating cases. I need clients to give me real information, not just what they think I want to hear. I'm honest with them and expect them to be honest with me. That helps me build stronger cases based on facts, not wishful thinking.

The truth is, our legal system isn't really about justice - it's about dispute resolution. I tell clients this upfront. We're not looking for vindication; we're looking for compensation and accountability. Understanding this helps keep expectations realistic and focuses energy on what we can actually achieve.

Because at the end of the day, my job isn't to tell clients what they want to hear. My job is to help them get results. Sometimes that means saying "I don't know." Sometimes it means saying "I can't help." But when I take a case, it means I believe in it and I'm ready to fight for it.

Sometimes these honest assessments lead to difficult conversations. I've had clients get angry when I tell them I can't take their case, or that their situation, while unfair, doesn't create a legal claim we can win.

I understand that anger. When you've been wronged by the system, hearing "I can't help" is incredibly frustrating, especially from someone you hoped would fight for you.

But I've learned that these tough conversations, while painful in the moment, serve everyone better in the long run. False hope doesn't help anyone. That said, I always encourage people to get a second opinion from another attorney. I'm not infallible - I miss things sometimes. If another lawyer spots something I didn't and finds a way to help someone I turned down, that's a win in my book. I'm happy to be proven wrong when it means someone gets the help they need. Because at the end of the day, this work isn't about me or my ego - it's about getting results for people who've been wronged by the system.

6

CHAPTER

FIGHTING BACK: LEGAL OPTIONS AND STRATEGIES

Understanding Your Legal Tools

The legal system gives you multiple ways to fight back when your rights are violated in prison. But choosing the right tool for your situation can mean the difference between winning and losing your case.

If someone's holding you past your release date, you might have:

- A state civil rights claim under the New Mexico Civil Rights Act
- A federal civil rights claim under Section 1983
- Claims under the New Mexico Tort Claims Act
- Standard tort claims against private entities
- An IPRA claim if they won't provide records
- A habeas corpus petition in some cases

Each of these tools has different strengths and requirements. Let me break them down in plain language.

The Game-Changer: New Mexico Civil Rights Act

The New Mexico Civil Rights Act, passed in 2021, completely changed how we fight these cases. Here's why it matters:

First, it removed qualified immunity as a defense. Before this law, prison officials could often dodge responsibility by claiming they weren't sure if what they were doing was wrong. They'd say, "Well, there's no previous case exactly like this one, so how could we know?" It was a get-out-of-jail-free card that made cases nearly impossible to win.

The Civil Rights Act ended that game. No more complicated immunity defenses. No more arguing about whether the right was "clearly established." Just the basic question: Did they violate your rights?

Remember Julie's case? Under the old system, the prison might have argued they weren't sure exactly how quickly they needed to process her release paperwork. Under the Civil Rights Act, that excuse doesn't work. They held her without legal authority - that's a violation, period.

The main limitations? Damages are capped at $2 million, and you can't get punitive damages. But for most cases, that's a fair trade-off for avoiding qualified immunity.

Federal Claims: Understanding the Trade-offs

When you bring a federal civil rights case under Section 1983, you're playing by a different set of rules than state claims. There's no cap on damages, and you can even get punitive damages if the conduct was particularly awful - but you're also facing bigger hurdles. You need every single juror to agree with you (not just ten out of twelve like in state court), you have to deal with qualified immunity (which means showing the violation was "clearly established" in previous cases), and federal courts tend to be tougher on civil rights cases overall. It's a trade-off: bigger potential rewards, but a steeper climb to get there.

Here's a practical reality: Most New Mexico civil rights lawyers prefer to avoid federal court when possible.

State court also lets us argue that the New Mexico Constitution provides greater protections than the U.S. Constitution. That means we can push for higher standards - better medical care, better conditions, stronger protections against abuse. We don't get that flexibility in federal court.

Tort Claims: A Two-Track System

When someone's rights are violated in prison, we often have two different types of tort claims available:

Standard Tort Claims:

These are basic civil claims anyone can bring when they're wronged:

- Can be brought against private entities (like prison contractors)
- No special notice requirements
- Three-year statute of limitations
- No cap on damages

Claims Under the Tort Claims Act

The New Mexico Tort Claims Act creates special rules for suing government entities:

- Must give notice within 90 days of the incident
- Two-year statute of limitations
- Damages are capped
- Only certain types of claims are allowed
- Special immunity provisions apply

Here's why understanding these differences matters: Let's say someone's held past their release date in a private prison. We might be able to bring:

- Standard tort claims against the private operator
- Tort Claims Act claims against state agencies
- Civil rights claims against both
- IPRA claims if they won't provide records

Each type of claim has different deadlines and requirements. Miss the 90-day notice for a Tort Claims Act claim? We can still pursue the others. Private operator claiming they deserve government protections? We can argue they don't get those protections since they're profiting from the activity.

The Power of Multiple Claims

Here's something crucial I've learned: Don't put all your eggs in one basket. When I file these cases, I often bring multiple types of claims based on the same incident. Why? Because different claims have different strengths.

Take Vincent's case. He was arrested by parole officers (state actors), held in a county jail, then transferred to a private prison. We brought civil rights claims against everyone involved (including the private prison – it was acting "under color of state law"), Tort Claims Act claims against government agencies, standard tort claims against private entities, and several IPRA claims for failure to turn over supporting documents.

This multilayered approach meant that if one claim had problems, we had backup options. When different entities started pointing fingers at each other, we could hold all of them accountable under different legal theories.

The Exhaustion Requirement

Here's a critical point that trips up many cases: For civil rights claims filed by prisoners who are still in custody, you have to "exhaust administrative remedies" before you can sue. In plain language, that means you need to:

1. File grievances about the problem
2. Appeal those grievances if they're denied
3. Follow all the deadlines in the grievance process

This is why I emphasized grievances so much in earlier chapters. If you don't handle this step correctly, you might lose your right to sue entirely. I've seen strong cases thrown out simply because someone didn't file the right grievances first. It doesn't matter how the violation of rights was, this requirement can destroy a claim unless the prisoner was somehow physically incapable or prevented from filing the grievance.

Making Strategic Choices

The key to using these tools effectively is understanding what you're trying to achieve. Are you primarily seeking:

- Release from custody?
- Compensation for illegal detention?
- Changes in prison policies?
- Some combination of these?

Your goals help determine which legal tools make the most sense. For example, if you're still being held illegally, a habeas corpus petition might be your fastest route to freedom. But if you're seeking compensation for past illegal detention, civil rights claims are usually the better path. In the right case, we may bring both at the same time.

This is why I spend so much time investigating cases before deciding how to proceed. I need to understand not just what went wrong, but which legal tools give us the best chance of fixing it.

Remember: The system has lots of tools to hold people in prison. But the law also gives us tools to fight back when they abuse that power. The key is knowing which tool to use and when to use it.

Understanding Habeas Corpus: Your Path to Freedom

Let me tell you about Michael's case, because it shows exactly what habeas corpus can do when used right.

Michael was young - still a child in the eyes of the law - when he was arrested and took responsibility for some very serious charges. He entered a plea agreement offered by the state. The court sentenced him as an adult, imposing a parole term of five to twenty years. Under the law, the parole board was supposed to hold hearings starting at the five-year mark to decide if Michael should stay on parole.

But here's what actually happened: The parole board just decided they didn't have to hold those hearings. Period. No legal basis - they just didn't do it. By the time I got involved, Michael had been in custody for about seventeen years.

When I reviewed his case, I found something even more shocking. That extended parole term that had kept him in prison for most of his adult life? It wasn't even legal. The plea agreement he signed never mentioned it. This matters because the law is crystal clear: A criminal defendant has the right to know what sentence they're agreeing to when they take a plea.

This is exactly what habeas corpus is for - when someone's being held illegally and needs a judge to step in. Think of habeas corpus as your emergency brake when the system's gone off the rails. The term literally comes from Latin phrases meaning "illegal holding of the body."

Here's what makes habeas different from other legal tools:

- It's focused on getting you released, not getting compensation
- It often moves faster than regular civil cases
- You can bring evidence that wasn't in your original case
- You can challenge things that happened after your conviction
- You're directly asking a judge to order your release

But habeas has its own strict rules:

- You generally have to exhaust your other remedies first, including direct appeal
- You need to show a fundamental problem with your detention
- You can't just rehash issues from your appeal
- You need new evidence or legal arguments

In Michael's case, I filed a habeas petition challenging his sentence. We won - the judge agreed the extended parole term was illegal because it wasn't in his plea agreement. Then we negotiated a new plea that didn't include the five-to-twenty years of parole.

But let me be really clear about something: Habeas isn't a magic wand. You can't use it just because you think your sentence is unfair or you don't like how the prison's treating you. You need to show a fundamental legal problem with your detention.

Here are the most common types of habeas claims:

- Illegal sentences (like Michael's case)
- Ineffective assistance of counsel
- New evidence of innocence
- Important constitutional violations that weren't raised on appeal
- Problems with how your sentence is being calculated or served

In one case I handled on appeal, the public defender told the judge she wasn't ready for trial and that she'd be constitutionally ineffective if forced to proceed. The judge made her go to trial anyway, and the appeals court affirmed. That's the kind of issue that might support a habeas claim - a clear constitutional violation that the regular appeals process didn't fix.

Habeas is powerful because it lets you go directly to a judge and say "I'm being held illegally - here's why." But that power comes with responsibility. You need to be thorough, precise, and able to prove exactly how your detention violates the law.

This is why documentation matters so much. In Michael's case, we could show the violation through the original plea agreement and audio recordings of the plea hearing. Together these proved that nobody fixed the issue.

When you can lay out that kind of evidence, habeas gives you a real shot at freedom. But you have to do it right. These cases often fail because people try to handle them without understanding the legal requirements. They throw everything at the wall hoping something sticks, instead of focusing on specific legal violations they can prove.

The bottom line is this: If you're being held illegally, habeas corpus might be your fastest path to freedom. But you need to be strategic about it. Focus on clear legal violations. Gather solid evidence. And understand that while habeas is powerful, it's also technical. Getting help from someone who knows these cases can make the difference between freedom and frustration.

Habeas Corpus vs. Direct Appeals: Understanding the Difference

Let me use my experience from both sides of the system to explain this. When I was handling appeals for the Attorney General's office and later for the Public Defender, I saw firsthand how these two tools serve completely different purposes.

Direct Appeals: Your First Shot at Review

A direct appeal is your first chance to challenge what happened in your case. Think of it like an instant replay in sports - you're asking a higher court to look at what happened and spot the errors. But here's the key limitation: You can only point to things that are already in the trial record. That means:

- Legal errors by the judge
- Problems with evidence
- Mistakes in jury instructions
- Issues your lawyer raised during trial

The catch? If it's not in the trial transcript, the appeals court can't consider it. No new evidence. Period.

Habeas Corpus: Your Safety Net

Habeas is different. It's for catching problems that either:

- Don't show up in the trial record,
- Happened after your conviction, including new evidence of actual innocence or important changes in controlling law, or
- Involve clear constitutional violations that weren't fixed on direct appeal.

Remember Michael's case? His extended parole term wasn't mentioned in his plea agreement - that's something we could prove with evidence outside the trial record. A direct appeal couldn't have fixed that problem because the issue wasn't visible in the original court proceedings.

Here are some other crucial differences:

Timing

- Direct Appeal: Must be filed quickly after sentencing (usually 30 days)
- Habeas: Can be filed later, but watch out for deadlines, including crucial differences between federal and state procedures. The interactions between state and federal habeas timing can be complicated – your best bet is always to talk to an attorney.

What You Can Challenge

- Direct Appeal: Errors that happened during your criminal case
- Habeas: Broader issues including:
  - How your sentence is being carried out
  - New evidence
  - Ineffective assistance of counsel
  - Constitutional violations that weren't visible at trial

Think of direct appeals and habeas as different tools in your toolbox. Appeals are for fixing mistakes that happened in court. Habeas is for problems that either weren't visible then or happened later. Knowing which tool fits your situation can make the difference between freedom and frustration.

Working with Multiple Defendants: Navigating Complex Cases

Let me show you how these cases often work in practice, using Vincent's case as an example. Think about what happened: A parole officer arrested him without authority, a county jail took him without paperwork, and a private prison accepted his transfer without checking if it was legal. That's three different entities, all playing a part in violating his rights.

Here's what makes these cases tricky: Everyone starts pointing fingers at everyone else. The parole officer says they were just following procedure. The jail says they trusted the parole officer's word. The private prison says they assumed the transfer was proper. Meanwhile, someone is sitting in a cell illegally.

So how do we handle this? First, we have to understand who's actually responsible for what:

- State agencies (like corrections and parole) operate under state authority
- County jails have their own policies and chain of command
- Private prisons are contractors trying to claim government protections
- Sometimes federal authorities are involved too

Each of these entities has different rules, different immunities, and different ways they can be held accountable. But here's what I've learned: Instead of letting them play the blame game, we often need to hold all of them responsible.

In Vincent's case, we brought:

- Claims against the state for the parole officer's actions
- Claims against the county for accepting him without proper authority
- Claims against the private prison for continuing his illegal detention
- Different types of claims against each one based on their role

Why? Because each entity had a chance to stop this train wreck and didn't. Each one had a duty to check whether they had legal authority to hold Vincent. None of them did.

Here's a practical example of how this plays out: When the private prison operator tried claiming they should get the same protections as state agencies, we pushed back hard. They're making a profit from incarceration - why should they get special government protections? Meanwhile, we made sure we had filed proper tort claims notices for the government entities within that crucial 90-day window.

The key is understanding that these entities often have overlapping responsibilities. Instead of trying to untangle who's most at fault, we often need to show how they all failed in their duties. Because at the end of the day, what matters isn't who's most responsible - it's getting justice for someone who was held illegally.

Putting a Price on Lost Freedom: The Challenge of Damages

Let me start with the basics: In law, when we talk about "damages," we're talking about money awarded to compensate someone who has been wronged. It's the legal system's way of trying to make things right - or at least as right as money can make them. Think of damages as the law's version of saying "we recognize you were hurt, and here's compensation to help address that harm." Sometimes calculating damages is straightforward, like fixing a damaged car or covering medical bills. But in civil rights cases, especially when someone's been held in prison past their release date, putting a dollar value on that harm gets complicated. Here's how we think about it:

When someone's held past their release date, there's no simple formula for calculating what that's worth. Unlike a car crash where we can add up medical bills, we're dealing with something more fundamental: the theft of someone's freedom. Every day someone spends illegally locked up is a day of life they can never get back - missed holidays with family, lost job opportunities, the basic human dignity of being free to make their own choices.

The law recognizes several categories of damages in these cases, and we work to tell our client's story through each of them:

First, there's basic compensation for the illegal detention itself. Courts have recognized that every day of wrongful imprisonment deserves compensation, sometimes as much as $1,000 per day. This isn't about specific losses - it's about the fundamental value of freedom. Think about it: what's it worth to spend an extra month in prison when you should be free? To miss your kid's birthday? To lose a job opportunity you had lined up?

Then we look at emotional distress and mental anguish. Take Jimmy's case. He was supposed to be home for Christmas. Instead, he sat in a cell watching the holiday pass, not knowing when he'd get out, unable to be with his children during a time that should have been filled with joy. That uncertainty - wondering if you've been forgotten by the system - takes a real psychological toll.

We also consider actual financial losses. Maybe you had a job lined up that you lost. Maybe your family had to pay for phone calls and commissary longer than they should have. Maybe you missed out on education or training opportunities. These concrete losses add up.

But here's what really moves these cases forward: telling our clients' stories. What was it like checking off days on a calendar past your release date, not knowing if anyone was even working on your paperwork? What opportunities slipped away while you waited? What did it feel like watching your family struggle without you when you should have been home helping?

This human element often proves more powerful than any mathematical calculation. Yes, we work within the legal framework - we can bring in experts to testify about psychological trauma or lost opportunities. But at its core, these cases are about reminding everyone involved - judges, juries, prison officials - that we're dealing with real people whose time and freedom have real value. When we can show not just that someone was held too long, but what that extra time actually cost them in human terms, that's when we get results.

Every extra day in prison is a day someone can never get back. Our job is to make sure the system recognizes that loss - not just with words, but with meaningful compensation that acknowledges the real human cost of illegal detention. It's about holding the system accountable and reminding everyone involved that prisoners' time and dignity matter just as much as anyone else's.

The Discovery Process: Getting to the Truth

Once a case is in litigation, we have powerful tools to uncover what really happened. Let me walk you through how we use the discovery process to build these cases.

Written Discovery:

First, we use written discovery - questions and document requests that defendants must answer under oath. I've learned to file these right away with the complaint. Why? Because I want to start building our case immediately and see any contrary evidence early.

Here's what we typically ask for:

- All records related to the detention
- Internal communications about the incident
- Policies and procedures
- Personnel files of involved staff
- Training materials
- Similar incidents in the past

But here's the key: We're not just fishing. By the time we file suit, we usually know what exists because of our pre-litigation investigation. We're often asking for specific documents we've already identified through IPRA requests or client record and using the records we already have to force important admissions.

Depositions:

Depositions are where we really dig into what happened. We get to question witnesses under oath, with a court reporter recording everything. This is crucial because:

- People have to answer our questions directly
- They can't hide behind written statements
- We can follow up on evasive answers
- Their testimony is locked in for trial

The Power of Rule 30(B)(6):

One of our most powerful tools is Rule 30(B)(6), which lets us depose an organization's designated representative. This means we can force an agency or prison to put someone forward who must testify about:

- How release dates are calculated
- What procedures should have been followed
- Why policies weren't followed
- Who was responsible for what

Here's why this matters: They can't just send someone to say "I don't know." The organization has to prepare their representative to testify about these topics. When they can't explain why they held someone illegally, that's powerful evidence because under the rules, the designated representative's testimony is binding on the agency.

Settlement or Trial: Making Choices That Matter

Let me be direct about something: The decision to settle or go to trial always belongs to the client. It's their case, their life, their future. My job is to help them make an informed choice by laying out the options clearly.

I evaluate every case based on the hard facts - what we can prove, what we learned in discovery, how similar cases have turned out, and what risks we face at trial. But this isn't just about calculating odds. When someone's been held illegally, when their rights have been violated, there's an emotional weight to these decisions that can't be measured in pure dollars and cents.

Many of our cases go through mediation, where both sides meet with a neutral mediator to explore settlement. I've found that mediation works best when we come thoroughly prepared with our evidence and when clients understand this is their chance to take control of the outcome. Having a skilled mediator can help cut through posturing and get to real solutions. Some of New Mexico's best mediators are retired judges who have presided over hundreds of trials and know what juries are likely to think and do.

When I advise clients about settlement offers, I'm looking beyond just what a jury might award if everything goes perfectly. We have to consider the risks of trial, how long it might take to get there, whether an appeal might follow. But most importantly, I'm thinking about what this resolution means for their life.

In Julie's case, the settlement we reached wasn't just about compensating her for those extra months in prison. It was about giving her resources to build a new life, to create opportunities that incarceration had taken away. When we discussed the settlement offer, we talked as much about her plans for the future as we did about the amount itself.

I've learned that for most clients, settlement isn't just about the money. It's about closing a painful chapter in their lives. It's about having the system finally acknowledge that what happened to them was wrong. Michael, who I mentioned earlier, got his GED in prison and wants to start his own business. That's what this work is really about - helping people move forward.

Sometimes the right choice is to fight it out at trial. If the system's conduct was egregious and they won't make a fair offer, we'll take our chances with a jury. As a former prosecutor, I'm always ready for that battle. But more often, the right choice is a settlement that gives certainty and closure. That lets someone start planning for what comes next instead of reliving what went wrong and spending years waiting for the case to make its way through the court system.

When we're making these decisions, I make sure my clients understand exactly what their options are, including all the risks and potential rewards. I explain my recommendation and my reasoning, but I always emphasize that the final decision is entirely theirs. Whether they choose to settle or go to trial, I'll support their choice and fight for them either way.

Because at the end of the day, this isn't just about resolving a legal case. It's about helping someone turn the page and start writing their next chapter. When I see former clients building better lives using their settlement money, starting businesses, supporting their families - that's when I know we've achieved something that matters. The system took away their freedom illegally; our job is to help them build something new with the compensation we secure for that wrong.

7

CHAPTER

BEYOND INDIVIDUAL CASES: WHY FOLLOWING RULES MATTERS

The Rule of Law Isn't Optional

If we lose the rule of law, we lose everything. I don't mean that as some abstract legal theory. I mean it as a practical reality I see play out in New Mexico's prisons again and again.

My experience has taught me something crucial about the rule of law - it's not just for corporate boardrooms and federal courthouses. It matters most in the places where power meets ordinary people.

Think about what the rule of law really means. It means that rules apply to everyone - not just to people without power, but to people with power too. It means that when a judge orders someone's release, that order isn't a suggestion. When someone's sentence is complete, they go home - not when it's convenient for the prison, not when the paperwork gets processed, but when their time is done.

But here's what I see happening in New Mexico's prisons: Officials treating the law like a buffet, picking and choosing which rules they'll follow. They hold people past release dates because paperwork is inconvenient. They ignore judges' orders because they disagree with them. They put people in solitary without proper hearings because it's easier than following procedure.

That's not just wrong - it's dangerous. Because if we accept that some people or agencies can ignore rules whenever they want, then we don't really have laws. We just have power. And a system based purely on power isn't a justice system at all.

Here's why this matters beyond any individual case: When we put someone in prison, we're saying that breaking society's rules has consequences. That's the whole basis for our justice system. But if the system itself won't follow rules - if prison officials can ignore judges, if release dates don't matter, if constitutional rights disappear behind prison walls - then we're not teaching respect for law. We're teaching that rules only matter when you lack power to ignore them.

When Individual Cases Create Bigger Change

Take what happened with the Parole Board and the New Mexico Corrections Department. For years, they made it difficult if not impossible to get records. You'd file a request under the public records law, and they'd just ignore it. When I started investigating cases, I couldn't even get basic documents about parole decisions.

So we started filing lawsuits - not just about the underlying civil rights violations, but about their failure to provide records. One case at a time, we forced them to pay settlements for violating the records law. Eventually, they completely changed how they handle records requests.

Or look at what happened after Jimmy's case. When the prison ignored his release order, we didn't just file a lawsuit - we went to the media. The next day's headline in the Albuquerque Journal read: "NM man still in prison despite judge's order." Suddenly, prison officials who'd been dragging their feet for weeks found the urgency to act. Jimmy went home the next day.

But here's what really matters: The next time the Corrections Department got a letter from my office that somebody was past their discharge date—the department acted.

Making the System Care

I've learned something crucial doing this work: Most problems in the system don't come from malice - they come from indifference. The parole officer who ignored the judge's release order in Vincent's case probably wasn't trying to be cruel. They just didn't care enough to handle it properly.

That's why these cases matter beyond just getting compensation for one person. Every case we win makes the system care a little more about following its own rules. Every settlement shows there's a cost to ignoring people's rights. Every time we prove that paperwork matters, that court orders can't be ignored, that release dates mean something - we're making the system work more like it's supposed to.

Real change in the prison system doesn't come from meetings or policy papers. It comes from making it more expensive to break the rules than to follow them.

I learned this running my own firm. Early on, I made a choice that shaped everything about how we work: I decided to invest serious time investigating cases before we take them. That means we turn down a lot of potential cases. But when we do take one, we've already found the evidence to prove exactly what went wrong and who's responsible.

My firm's approach is pretty simple: We look for cases where we can prove the system broke its own rules. Not just complaints about tough conditions or unfair treatment, but clear violations we can document:

- Release dates ignored
- Court orders not followed
- Rights violated despite clear rules saying otherwise

We investigate thoroughly before we file anything. When we bring a case, we've already:

- Gathered all the key records
- Found the internal communications
- Documented who knew what and when
- Built evidence that will hold up in court

This isn't just about winning cases - it's about making the system work like it's supposed to. Every settlement creates pressure to fix the underlying problems. Every case we win makes it harder for them to ignore the next person's rights.

Why This Work Matters

When we win a settlement for someone who was held past their release date or subjected to illegal conditions, we're not just getting them compensation for what happened. We're giving them tools to build something new. Maybe that's starting a small business when they get out. Maybe it's having a place to live instead of starting from nothing. Maybe it's being able to help their family and show they're more than their worst mistakes.

I believe in this work because I've seen how it changes lives. Not just by holding the system accountable, but by giving people real chances to rebuild. When a former client tells me they've started a business with their settlement money, or they're finally getting proper medical care, or they're able to help their kids - that's when I know we've achieved something that matters.

The system took away their freedom illegally. Our job is to help them build something new with the compensation we secure for that wrong. One client, one case, one new chapter at a time.

WHAT HAPPENS WHEN NO ONE FOLLOWS THE RULES

When the system holds someone past their release date, it's not just breaking rules - it's shattering the basic promise of justice in America. Think about what it really means: The government is taking someone's freedom without any legal authority. In a country founded on constitutional rights, that's supposed to be impossible.

But it happens in New Mexico's prisons. Not rarely. Not by accident. It happens because people in power decide that some rules don't matter, that some court orders can be ignored, that some people's freedom isn't worth the paperwork.

A judge orders someone released, but the prison doesn't act. Someone's sentence is complete, but their paperwork sits on a desk. A parole officer decides they know better than a court. Each time, someone sits in a cell illegally while their family waits, while their life is on hold, while the system treats their freedom like an inconvenience.

This isn't just wrong - it's dangerous to everything we believe about justice. The whole idea of rule of law means that no one is above the rules. Not the people we put in prison, but also not the people who run the prisons. Not the inmates who broke society's laws, but also not the officials who ignore court orders.

That's why I've built my practice the way I have. When I investigate cases, I'm not just looking for violations - I'm gathering proof that the system knowingly broke its own rules. When I file lawsuits, I'm not just seeking compensation - I'm forcing them to face consequences for treating people's rights as optional.

Every settlement we win does two things: It helps one person rebuild their life, and it makes it more expensive for the system to ignore the next person's rights. Every case we prove sends a message that treating freedom casually has costs. Every time we force them to follow their own rules, we move a little closer to having a justice system worthy of the name.

I'll keep fighting these battles because the alternative is accepting that some people's rights don't matter. That the government can take freedom without authority. That the constitution is just words on paper. That's not justice - it's just power pretending to be law.

And in America, we're supposed to be better than that.

Getting Help: What We Need From You

If you or your loved one is facing issues with illegal detention, here's how to reach out to my firm effectively:

First Contact:

- If you are in custody, write a letter explaining the situation. Be specific about dates, facilities, and what's happened. Include any documents. Don't attempt to schedule a legal call if we've never heard from you before – we receive too many inquiries to schedule calls without some information about what's going. We need to review documents first to help effectively, and we never give legal advice unless it's through a scheduled, confidential legal call.

- If you are in custody and there's an urgent issue, the best method is to have friends or family members call us or contact us through the website.

- If you are in custody and there are no other options, call and let us know you're being illegally detained and need a legal call. Don't provide any other information (and don't expect us to provide any advice) on a monitored line. Confidential information should only be shared during a scheduled, confidential legal call.

- If you are out of custody, feel free to write, call, or contact us through the website.

Key Documents We Need:

- Judgment and sentence from the court
- Any recent court orders
- Good time figuring sheets
- Disciplinary records
- Grievances filed about the issue

- Any responses from prison officials
- Records of attempts to resolve the problem
- Medical records if they're relevant

How to Organize Materials:

- Make copies of everything - never send originals
- Put documents in chronological order
- Include a timeline of important events
- Don't use staples – it makes it harder for to scan and process the documents

Remember: The more organized your information is, the faster we can evaluate your case. We investigate thoroughly before taking cases because we only want to file claims we can prove.

Contact us at:

Stalter Law LLC
PO Box 90336
Albuquerque, NM 87199
(505) 315-8370
www.stalterlaw.com
www.nmprisonbook.com

What to Expect:

- We'll review your materials carefully
- We may request additional documents
- We'll be direct about whether we can help

- If we can't take your case, we'll try to explain why
- If we do take your case, we'll explain exactly what happens next

Our process might seem thorough, but it's designed to get results. We take cases seriously because freedom is serious. If you're reaching out to us, something has already gone wrong. Our job is to figure out if we can make it right.

Remember, because of my firm's reputation, people bring us far more cases than we can take. If we decline your case, it doesn't necessarily mean you don't have a case. There's a good chance it just wasn't the right fit for our firm. Always get second, third, or even fourth opinions from other law firms.

A FINAL NOTE

The information in this book is meant to help you understand your rights and options, but it's not a substitute for legal advice. Every case is different, and the law changes over time. If you believe your rights have been violated, don't try to figure it out alone - talk to a qualified attorney who can look at your specific situation and tell you where you stand.

The stories and examples in this book show what's possible, but only a lawyer who knows the details of your case can tell you what might work for you. Use this book as a starting point for understanding the system but remember that protecting your rights requires proper legal help.

Stalter Law LLC
PO Box 90336
Albuquerque, NM 87199
(505) 315-8370
www.stalterlaw.com
www.nmprisonbook.com